Cultivating A Motivated Mindset

Cultivating A Motivated Mindset

8 Actions Steps to Developing

a Motivated Mind

By: Ydrate "The Motivator" Nelson, M. Ed

Copyright © 2022 by Ydrate Nelson & Associates LLC/ BE THE GREATEST Publishing.

All rights reserved. No part of this publication may be reproduced, distributed, or transmitted in any form or by any means, including photocopying, recording, or other electronic or mechanical methods, without the prior written permission of the publisher, except in the case of brief quotations embodied in critical reviews and specific other noncommercial uses permitted by copyright law. For permission requests, write to the publisher, addressed "Attention: Permissions Coordinator," Ydrate Nelson/ BE THE GREATEST. Publishing

3101 N. Central Ave Suite 183 #760

Phoenix, Arizona 85004

Book Layout ©2022 Ydrate Creates Design/Ydrate The Motivator Nelson

Book Cover Design J. Daniels

Book Editor Dr. Sharon Michael-Chadwell
—1st ed.

ISBN 978-0-9860929-3-0

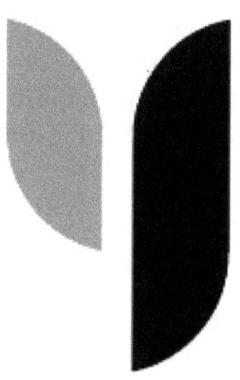

Table of Contents

Preface vi

Introduction xiii

Maximizing The Book xv

Chapter 1: Believe In Yourself…#Doubelieve 1

Chapter 2: Adopt A Positive Mindset 13

Chapter 3: Find Your Why & Set A Goal 25

Chapter 4: Master Focus Management 37

Chapter 5: Do Not Compromise 47

Chapter 6: Find Your Motivated Tribe 58

Chapter 7: Take Breaks When Necessary 69

Chapter 8: Keep Trying. Don't Give Up 80

Conclusion: 96

BE THE GREATEST Bonus Resources 97

Preface

This book went from a tool intended for the benefit of other people to a literal resource to help me deal with some of the most challenging days of my life. I wrote this book in 2020 during the pandemic to be a tool I could use to motivate the 200 high school students I was teaching at West Point High School in Arizona. I wanted this book to be a resource my fellow teachers could use to keep themselves and their students motivated and inspired. I intended for this book to be a tool that working professionals could use to live a more motivated and higher quality of life. I wanted this to be simple, relatable, and applicable.

In June of 2021, I was diagnosed with colon cancer. In July, I was upgraded to stage 4 after discovering cancer had spread to my liver. At that moment, this book became a tool full of resources to help keep my mind empowered to defeat cancer. I was preparing myself for the battle of my life, and my motivated mindset would be the key. In the end, it is my motivated mindset that continues to save my life. There were certain habits I had to form and break. If it were not for my motivated mindset, I would have quit.

My first trip to the Cancer Center was eye-opening. When I stepped into the building, I realized that I was fighting against cancer in my body and mind. When I walked in, I saw that many people were in the middle of the same battle I was beginning. I could see the hope and pain in the eyes of my fellow fighters and their families. I could feel the anxiety from dealing with the unknown. While having support is vital, I still had to face the lonely, personal, and individual fight against cancer…alone.

After consulting with my doctors about my treatment plan, I realized I had a true battle right before me. I was looking at months of chemotherapy and scheduled surgery times in the months ahead. I was facing a ton of adversity. I was about to go somewhere I had never imagined in my life. It was time to prepare my mind for the battle that my body was about to face. It was finally time for me to place the lessons in this book to work and share my personal experience alongside the results, hoping it would be helpful to others.

Below, you will find the digital link that will direct you to this book. The QR code will be updated when the 2.0 version is available, and you can enjoy the additional content and valuable information.

Scan the code and get the most recent version of Cultivating A Motivated Mindset.

As new versions are released, the link will be updated.

Enjoy your journey as you Cultivate your Motivated Mindset.

Introduction

No matter what you desire to achieve in this life, a certain mindset goes along with reaching any goal. Your destination is attached to your mindset, whether intentional or unintentional. No matter the outcome, good, bad, or indifferent, mindset plays a role in the results of your day-to-day life.

That mindset doesn't appear. It must be cultivated. Your mindset must be developed over a period to form the proper habits. Without taking charge to take control of your life, you leave it up to chance. This book is a resource to help you on your journey to create a better way of thinking.

Cultivate – Prepare to use for crops or gardening.

When I was a kid in Dublin, Georgia, I had the privilege of being around my Grandmother and Grandfather. They both had a unique set of skills. My Grandmother was more than just a cook; she was a culinary genius. My Grandfather, who came from a sharecropping background, was more than just a farmer; he was an agricultural engineer. As a child growing up, he grew most of the food we ate in the garden right outside.

We had all the vegetables and various fruits grow right in our front yard. We would always have fresh food in the spring and freeze the surplus for the winter. The food we grew in our yard included cabbage, greens, peas, corn, butter beans, tomatoes, onions, peppers, watermelon, cantaloupe, and sugar cane, to name a few. We got it out of the mud.

I remember my Grandfather would spend weeks and the days leading up to the planting season preparing the ground for use. He would plow the field and turn over the soil. He would take the time to map out the rows and plan what would go where. Each item had its place. He took time to cultivate and prepare the ground for gardening.

My Grandmother would then take the fruits of my Grandfather's labor and turn them into daily meals that nourished our family physically and spiritually. My Grandmother would create excellent daily meals; she would go through a process to prepare our food. She would make homemade biscuits and cakes from scratch. She made homemade preserves and prepared all the different animals my Grandfather would deliver.

We also raised our animals, including my pet goat; each was used for food. The animals we ate from our yard or garden included chickens, pigs, squirrels, possums, raccoons, rabbits, deer, and fresh fish from the pond across the street. I had the pleasure of watching my Grandmother prepare each of these items consistently. As she prepared each item, each had its separate process and had to be prepared and cultivated in a certain way before it could be used.

When I speak of cultivation, it is in the context of getting the ground of your mind ready to plant seeds of motivation. I am speaking of finding the right process to get you one step closer to your Greatness. Nothing just happens overnight. Everything must be cultivated over time, including your mind.

Motivation is derived from the Latin word *movere,* which means to move. So, at the base of motivation is movement.

Motivation is at the foundation of personal and organizational success. American experimental psychologist and inventor Paul Thomas defined motivation as generating action, sustaining them, and regulating it (Young, 1961). When there is no motivation, there is no movement.

I remember being stuck with no movement. Back in 2005, I lost one of my close friends to homicide. He was gunned down as I was literally on the phone with his sister as it happened right outside their shared home. This person was someone I saw every day for 22 days straight, and he was killed the day I didn't see him.

The night before his demise, we met in my garage and discussed our plans. We mapped out what we wanted to do and how we intended to get there. Never did I think that would be our last conversation.

When Chris Wright left this world, I lost and lacked motivation. I was sad and even a bit depressed at times. The plans we shared were out the window, and everything changed.

I remember losing sight of what I wanted and how to get there.

I lost my job, and my car broke down. It was a low point. At one point, I didn't even want to get out of bed.

One night I woke up out of my sleep and realized that I was crying in my sleep. I was so sad and paranoid; I didn't want to live like this. I prayed to God and asked for help. I sat up in bed and just cried. I picked up a pen and wrote a poem, "At worst if I fall."

After writing, I realized I would fight hard to stay motivated and keep moving forward. My mind would be overcome with the world's negativity if I didn't.

I started a mindset transformation on that day to take action and live a motivated life. That is the journey that I am still on to this day. I think about my friend and brother daily and use his life to motivate me to greater heights. I won't stop moving.

Mindset is your mental attitude that determines how you interpret and respond to situations. Your mindset is developed and "cultivated" over some time. While there are many different types of mindsets, we focus on the motivated mindset needed for higher achievement in this book.

After I lost my friend Chris Wright, I had to go on a mindset transformation. I fought daily to stay on the right mental path. A few years later, I made a life-changing decision. I decided to move from Atlanta, Georgia, to Phoenix, Arizona. The day I left, I had a conversation with myself. I knew I would go to a new place where I had never lived and meet many new people. All the sadness and drama I was leaving behind and moving on. I was making a significant mindset shift.

I used the entire 30-hour drive to decompress my mind and just listen to my thoughts. I decided I was going to fast from anger and stress for as long as I could. I used a series of activities, including reciting poetry, listening to music, attending church, and meditating to fast from anger for over a year.

My journey to strengthen my mindset led me to the Southwest Institute of Healing Arts in Tempe, Arizona, where I completed my life coaching program to further develop my mind and the mindset of those I am called to serve.

As a coach, I am consistently inspired by those who choose me to partner with on their journey to Greatness. I am always looking for ways to serve my partners better as we work on mindset development.

I am still on my journey to develop and prepare my mind to take massive action needed for Greatness continuously. My journey has left a few clues and a blueprint to create a more motivated mindset. I want to share them with you in hopes that we can Cultivate A Motivated Mindset together.

"Cultivating A Motivated Mindset is the foundation to manifesting your Greatness."

Maximizing the Book

The best way to apply and maximize this book is to keep it simple. This book is written from a personal perspective followed by objective analysis. There is a coaching support question in each chapter. Answer the questions. For best results, write down each question and write out your answer. Use the Notes section at the end of the book to do the work.

There are also recommended actions after each set of questions. Write down the suggestion and do what you feel can help reinforce what you are seeking to do. Check your results, adjust, and repeat.

True change will not come from reading this book. True change comes from applying the principles and cultivating a motivated mindset over time. You can read this book in less than a day, but it will take time to apply the principles.

The Journey Begins.

If you want to develop and cultivate a motivated mindset to reach your Greatness, you have stumbled upon the right book.

This book is aimed directly at just that. It will help you learn how to create a motivated mindset in nature to elevate and BE THE GREATEST version of yourself. The goal is to gift you with mindset that will mentally elevate you and the people you encounter. Your life will completely turn around to benefit you and those you serve.

This volume is composed of eight chapters. Each chapter will teach you the necessary step you need to take, one by one, to own a motivated mind.

The volume starts with the first chapter that will tell you to believe in yourself before starting any task, as it is the most needed step and comes above any other step.

When you have induced trust in yourself, your work doesn't end there. To believe in yourself, you must also adopt a positive attitude towards life and your work life. Take on positive attributes that will help you advance towards your goal in the most optimistic way.

Now, it's time to act. Set goals for yourself that relate to what you want to do. Once you have done that, we move on to the third chapter. The third chapter will tell you how to implement your goals once you've set them.

The fourth chapter will give you an overview of how vital it is to stay focused on your goals. Setting up goals and actions are vital success steps. To make sure you stay on that path . . . you need to give it all your attention and devotion by staying focused.

With the fifth chapter, you will learn an important lesson. Be selfish when it comes to your goals. Do not ever compromise on them.

The sixth chapter tells you to spend time with non-toxic and motivated people only. This progress will help you motivate even more since your surroundings will be by your side as well.

Chapter seven reminds us to embrace rest. Overworking yourself is never good for anyone. So, take breaks when you need them. Don't ignore the need for breaks. It doesn't make you weak. It makes you more effective.

Finally, the last chapter assures you that failing is also a part of the process. Don't be discouraged and keep trying even if you fail. To succeed, you need to understand the value of failure.

The Conclusion is an introduction to The S.T.E.E.R. C.L.E.A.R. Method, a cognitive reconstruction tool used to help cultivate the mindset needed to maximize Greatness.

SOMETHING TO REMEMBER:

Believe in yourself. That's the secret sauce to your success.

NOW, GO BE THE GREATEST YOU.

CHAPTER 1

BELIEVE IN YOURSELF...#DoUBelieve

My Connection....

When I worked towards my dreams and goals, I found myself falling way short of where I felt I should be. I was investing in education, mentoring, coaching, and still not reaching the goals or my heart's desire. I was feeling a bit discouraged. I thought maybe it was not meant to be, or I should just give up on certain things.

I started to doubt myself and question my purpose. For years I thought, the key to my success was all about mindset. While I still believe this to be true, I discovered that my mindset alone was not enough. I found myself trying to figure out why I was still falling short. At the time I was missing the realization that I needed to align my mindset with my personal beliefs.

It took me some but finally, through years of studying, researching, and processing, I started to understand why I continued to fall short. I worked hard to cultivate my mindset guided by the 8 to 12 percent of my conscious brain. This is the space where I can consciously control my thoughts and daily decisions. This is home to my creativity and free thinking. This mindset that I put so much thought into was not enough.

In a lecture on his book the *Biology of Belief*, I heard Bruce Lipton state that the conscious mind can process information at about 40 bytes of information per second. I thought that was a great feat to be accomplished in such a short time.

Bruce Lipton stated that the subconscious could process information at millions of bytes per second. This knowledge was a profound realization for me.

The subconscious mind is the home and guides to my belief system, habits, mental programming, basic instincts, deepest thoughts, and emotions. This space is where my mind takes over and handles the things I am not even considering. The subconscious brain handles 88 to 92% of my brain's daily activity through instinct and programming.

When I accepted the thought that my subconscious mind is a million times stronger than my conscious mind, I started to understand how my subconscious mind will always dominate a challenge from my conscious mindset. That is like challenging my newborn son to a tug-a-war. Even if he was the strongest baby in the world, he is no match for the strength of a grown man.

I figured out the key to my success was to have my mindset and belief system work together. My positive mind could never compete with my programmed subconscious belief system. No matter what I think, a small amount of doubt in my programming could undermine my success.

My journey began and became the base for this chapter. It was formed of the thought—what can I do to strengthen my belief in myself and my goals?

What can we do?

My Objective Perspective.

The first and the most important step for whenever you want to begin doing something is to make yourself believe that you can do it.

It might sound cliché, but it is what you need. Before starting any task, it is important to take a deep breath and tell yourself that you can do it. There is nothing in this world that you can't do. You are fully capable of carrying out this task you are about to do, just the way you want. You can do it perfectly.

That inspirational talk is necessary for doing anything. If you first tell yourself that you can do something, it's more likely that you can. You will have put your trust in yourself. You will have believed in yourself. The task will be easier to do if your trust is in you.

Figuring out how to have confidence in yourself will open up unlimited conceivable outcomes in your day-to-day existence. Now and again, you may find this hard to do. We've been adapted for the duration of our lives to question ourselves. We should rearrange our minds so that we can get rid of self-doubt and welcome confidence.

Everything you achieve in your life comes from putting your trust in yourself and believing that you can do it.

"If you are going to believe, start with you."

To have confidence in yourself, you initially need to accept that what you need is conceivable.

Researchers used to accept that people reacted to data streaming into the mind from the rest of the world. Yet, we can be sure that all things considered, we react to what the mind — because of experience.

Indeed, the brain is quite an incredible instrument; I learned in the book *Think and Grow Rich* by Napoleon Hill that the brain can convey what you want in the form of inspiration and desire.

The importance of your desire lies in believing that you believe that what you want can do and will happen. This belief is a way of controlling your mind.

The capacity to put your belief in yourself can transform you.

Simply think:

Why might it matter in your life if you had steadfast trust in your capacity to accomplish anything you truly set your attention to?

What might you need, wish, and trust?

What might you hope against hope if you had confidence in yourself with such profound conviction that you had no apprehensions of disappointment at all?

The vast majority of people start with close to nothing or low fearlessness; independently, they become intense, daring, and active. If you overcome your fear and take the steps that other fearless people take, you will see that you will also get the same results as them.

The results can't be rushed. Being patient with yourself is how you can learn to trust yourself. Take it one step at a time and make use of your amazing and positive qualities. Let them do their magic, all the while believing in yourself.

Make sure to set some time aside to find out who you are so you can know where your confidence lies. Know thyself.

If you need to transform yourself by turning into a creator, accept that you can do it. For me, the hardest part of that excursion was finding the certainty to figure out how to compose a book. When you grasp a demonstrated framework to plan, produce, and distribute your work, the bigger objective gets simpler to accomplish.

By trusting yourself, you will discover the mental fortitude to quickly move on your objectives.

Repeat affirmations, for example, "I have confidence in and believe in myself," consistently.

Your thoughts become words, and your words become your activities. On the off chance that you keep on disclosing to yourself that you have faith in yourself, in the long run, you truly will put stock in yourself.

It's that basic.

Have the fearlessness to acknowledge yourself as you truly may be or as another person might suspect you should be—and realize that you are a very decent individual, mulling over everything.

We have our gifts, aptitudes, and capacities that make us uncommon.

Nobody, including yourself, knows of your capacities or of what you may, at last, do or turn into. Maybe the hardest activity in life is acknowledging how uncommon you truly can be. Have confidence in yourself; afterward, use this mindfulness to improve your mentality and character.

When you have confidence in yourself and comprehend what you're able to do, that is all you'll require. No scorn or recognition of your abilities from others will sufficiently be able to restrict your hidden capacity. Goodbye to the restrictions that business uses to hold you back mentally. You are your own conscious. Make your game plans so you can do significantly more than you think and way more than anyone would envision.

"Stay true to your authentic self, and it's all you truly have."

Trust yourself and believe that you can do whatever you set your mind to. Fight to put yourself into positive, winning situations. No one knows when an opportunity will come knocking, so stay alert. Always believe that you can and will do what is necessary when the time is right. Preparation is key.

Coaching Support Questions:

Remember that building self-confidence is an ongoing process, and journaling can be a powerful tool for self-reflection and personal growth. These questions can help you gain insight into your strengths, challenges, and progress along the way.

Reflect on Your Strengths:
- What are three qualities or skills that you believe make you unique or special?
- How have you used these strengths in the past to overcome challenges or achieve goals?
- What can you do today to further develop and leverage these strengths in your personal and professional life?

Setting and Celebrating Achievements:
- What are three short-term goals you can set for yourself right now, no matter how small they may seem?
- How will achieving these goals contribute to your overall self-confidence?
- After reaching each goal, take some time to reflect and celebrate your achievement. Write about how it made you feel and what you learned from the experience.

Challenging Self-Doubt:
- What are some common negative thoughts or self-doubts that arise when you face a new challenge or opportunity?
- Can you identify any patterns or triggers for these self-doubts?
- Write down a recent situation where you felt self-doubt. How did you handle it, and what positive affirmations or strategies could you employ in the future to counteract these doubts?

<u>Recommended Action</u> Item to help Build Self Confidence.

Overcoming Self Doubt- I, like most people, have some level of self-doubt. Self-doubt is a crimpling thought process that has killed more dreams than the lack of opportunity itself. When we have no or little self-confidence, the likelihood of achieving goals decreases tremendously. By building and believing in yourself, self-confidence will skyrocket as well as your greatest achievements. I would recommend helping to boost your confidence that you:

1. **Do something BOLD or new.** Expand your comfort zone and try something new and different. Now is the time to write that book or start that business. You could also start smaller and try new food, hairstyle, vacation spot, or outfit. Do something outside of your comfort zone and grow yourself. When you take bold actions, you build confidence.

2. *Write yourself a love letter-* It is easy for us to look at other people and what they have. When we compare ourselves to them, we can easily get discouraged and run into a wall of self-doubt that has an ultimate effect on our confidence.

When you take a step back and look at yourself without comparing yourself to others, you have a better chance to focus on your Greatness.

At that moment, I would recommend that you take the time to draft yourself a love letter. Highlight all of the great things about yourself and encourage yourself with your own words. Keep a copy and read it when you need an internal boost.

3. **Make a weekly grateful list-** We can all get caught up the somebody else's hype and forget to appreciate who we are and what we have. Take the time to write down some of the good things in your life and keep a perspective on how blessed you are. Even on your worst day, something is amazing to be thankful for. Don't miss the opportunity to build confidence by keeping in perspective the many things we can be great forceful.

What are you grateful for right now?

Declaration of Self Confidence.

I am neither afraid of the future nor ashamed of the past.

I accept the reality of my imperfections. I cannot change anything but my present mental state of mind.

I have turned my regrets into learning experiences. I am taking charge of my destiny.

I am taking control of my life by focusing my energies on consistently completing tasks guilt-free.

I learn to achieve by progressively growing and problem-solving to reach my ultimate goals.

No matter what obstacles come my way, I will count it all joy.

Integrity is the foundation of my vision and a structure to my ideas.

I am not looking in my tiny rear-view mirror, watching the past get further away.

I am looking through my big windshield, embracing all of the opportunities coming towards me.

I am moving forward in physical and mental progression. My arms are open wide, and I am ready to embrace Greatness and higher achievement.

I Believe in myself.

SOMETHING TO REMEMBER:

Life is going to present us all with some challenges. The key is to find a reason to put a smile on your face. There is always a reason to be grateful. There is always a reason to smile.

NOW, GO BE THE GREATEST YOU.

CHAPTER 2

ADOPT A POSITIVE MINDSET

My Connection....

Many people see me today and say you are always motivated and always positive. Many of them don't know about my struggles. They don't know about the days when I would wake up out of my sleep crying. They don't know about my depression and suicidal thoughts. All they see is the result. It was a journey. It is still a journey.

Most people don't see the work it took for me to get to this point. And even though I still have my struggles, finding a way to create more positive thoughts is at the forefront of my daily mission.

Realizing the power of my thoughts made me realize that many of us share the same struggles. When we don't embrace the benefits of positive thinking, it creates unnecessary obstacles. When I embraced positive thinking consistently, my life changed, and I began a whole new journey.

The reality is that I am fully aware of how hard life is. I know that life is not about superficial unicorns and rainbows. My previous adversities are the main reason I focus on developing a positive mind. I know more hard days are coming and by building up my mindset to embrace positive thinking, I am better prepared to deal with the inevitable. That reality drives my desire to be more positive.

When I was diagnosed with stage 4 cancer, the years of positive thinking paid off. While many people expected me to handle the situation like they would and fall victim to negative thinking, I embraced positive thinking even more. I was prepared for the adversity because I spent years building myself to deal with whatever potential challenge presented. I knew that positive thinking was a superpower that would help propel me beyond low-vibrating thoughts and actions.

I do firmly believe that if I didn't embrace positive thinking, cancer would have had a bigger advantage. As a result of the positive thought-building habits formed, I prepared for what was coming my way. I didn't wait until hard times hit. I was positive daily, which was a massive part of my cancer-fighting battles. There were many hard days, and many times, I felt afraid. There were even days when I questioned my ability to defeat cancer. Those were fleeting thoughts that got weaker because my mind was programmed always to think positively. When we learn how to harness the power of positive thinking, there is no limit to what we can accomplish. I want more people to join me on this journey to create a more positive mindset. We are all in this together.

"I would rather be naggingly positive than destructively negative, but that's just me."

My Objective Perspective...

It is very hard to find any disadvantages to having an inspirational demeanor and positive mindset throughout everyday life. In any event, being surrounded by people who are hopeful, thankful, and see adversity as a test instead of hopelessness, is revitalizing. It is vital that we not only become more positive but choose to be surrounded by the motivated.

A positive mindset can't be simply cultivated within yourself, but also within the environment in which you live. It has been proven that the consistent presentation of negative words won't simply influence your temperament. It will influence your profitability and your life expectancy. It might feel uncomfortable to ask your companions or associates to quit complaining and grumbling or to truly consider leaving the room if the whining doesn't stop. But, when other people whine, complain, and share negative energy, you are impacted whether you realize it or not. Create your own space, embrace the positive, and stay away from the negative.

A smile goes a long way in developing a more positive mindset. Smiling does not simply lessen pressure and help you to assemble more sure feelings, but at the same time, it's influencing others. I found that outward appearances are infectious, so if by chance you have an inspirational disposition to smile or grin at other people, you'll probably get a smile or grin back. Use your smile as a superpower to spread positive vibes.

To help create a more positive mindset, one of the best things you can do to turn into a self-confident motivated person is to be thankful. Recognizing that things aren't that terrible and being optimistic have an enormous effect on your day-by-day life.

In case you're not a self-confident person (yet), you will need to start programming your mind until you make it a reality. Use positive affirmations to program your mind for confidence. Confidence is key when faced with adversity.

There is always the possibility that "terrible" things may occur. If they occur, rethink your strategy, and reinforce your self-belief. Of course, in that second, you may think, "this is the only way," or "this was the best I will get." It is important to reframe all negative thoughts instantly. One thing prompts another, and an underlying "terrible" thing may prompt even more "terrible" things. The key is to stay confident in yourself and believe you can handle anything that comes your way.

> "The intensity of smiling is not about you but those who are impacted by your light. No matter what you do, **(SWAG.)** Smile While Always Grinding."

Positive thinkers possess a habit, which is never taking bad things personally. They always try to better a terrible situation. If they experience, for instance, an individual disappointment, they see it as a temporary situation and not a life sentence. The fact that something good is coming helps deal with the current "terrible" situation from a more positive perspective.

A similar action goes for good occasions— individuals don't rationalize if they prevail at something by feeling humiliated and saying, "Anyway, I just lucked out." They are cheerful about it and applaud what they have accomplished. They commend every little success because they prepared and were confident. You should do the same. Celebrate your hard work and accomplishments as fuel to keep your mindset focused.

Qualities of an inspirational mentality with a positive mindset; work to effectively build confidence, acknowledgment, versatility, appreciation, care, and respectability in your life. Each individual is responsible for creating the right formula that will assist you with cultivating and keeping up an uplifting attitude and positive mindset.

Building up a positive mindset and picking up the right mental habits are elements that require attention and intention to cultivate.

It will not happen overnight. Try not to stress or become impatient. Stay mission focused and locked in on the positive. This isn't about the sort of sure reasoning that everything is perfect because we are optimistic. We can't guarantee that just "indulging cheerful thoughts" will manifest all you want throughout the day or everyday life, but it does increase the likelihood of more positive results.

Building up a positive mindset isn't tied in with being continually glad or bright, and it's not tied in with overlooking anything negative or horrendous in your life. It's tied in with fusing both the positive and negative into your viewpoint and deciding to at present be commonly idealistic. When I was diagnosed with stage 4 colon cancer, I could not just smile and pretend it was not a serious situation. However, after realizing how serious my situation was, my mindset shifted to the fact that I was capable of beating cancer. My focus was on living and not dying and greeted each day of the challenge with a positive attitude because knew the hard that negativity has on mental and physical health.

We must accept that you won't generally be upbeat during the initial reception with "terrible news" or adversity. I can't pretend like

I was happy when I initially found out I had cancer. I was tasked with figuring out how to acknowledge negative thoughts, awful states of mind, and troublesome feelings when they come but also redirect them to more positive thinking. I always say you can't build a home where you should be pitching a tent. This means when you are hit with adversity, don't sit on the negative for too long. Redirect your thinking back to the positive and move past negative low vibrating thoughts. Build your home on a solid foundation of positive energy.

At the point when you decide to surrender to the cynicism, negativity, and pessimism perspective on the world, you are not just submitting to a deficiency of control and conceivably floundering in misery—you are passing up a significant open door for development and improvement. When you let go of the negative you create more space for positivity to flow through.

Building a positive structure for your mindset isn't tied in with being bubbly and annoyingly merry; however, it is about making an interest in yourself and your future. It's all right to feel down or think skeptically some of the time; yet, deciding to react with idealism, flexibility, and appreciation will benefit you undeniably more over the long haul. Keep cultivating a positive mindset.

Coaching Support Questions:

Gratitude and Appreciation:
- What are three things you are genuinely grateful for in your life right now, no matter how big or small?
- How do these things make you feel, and how can you express your appreciation for them?
- How might focusing on gratitude and appreciation daily influence your overall attitude and outlook on life?

_____
_____
_____
_____
_____
_____
_____
_____
_____
_____
_____
_____
_____
_____
_____
_____
_____

Daily Positivity Journal:
- At the end of each day, record three positive moments or experiences you had during the day.
- Reflect on how these moments made you feel and why they were significant.
- Over time, review your positivity journal to identify patterns and discover what consistently brings positivity into your life.

_____
_____
_____
_____
_____
_____
_____
_____
_____
_____
_____
_____
_____
_____
_____
_____
_____
_____

Positive Self-Talk:
- Pay attention to your self-talk throughout the day. Write down any negative or self-critical thoughts you notice.
- For each negative thought, challenge it with a positive or self-affirming statement. How does this change your perspective?
- What strategies can you implement to replace negative self-talk with positive and encouraging thoughts on a regular basis?

Recommended Action

1. Find a book of motivational or inspirational quotes, sign up for motivational quotes to be delivered via email or read your preferred scriptures daily to stimulate more positive thinking.

2. Create a list of the people who are in your motivated circle. If you don't have one, create one. Set up weekly accountability calls to help empower each other.

3. Create a journal to help you write down your positive thoughts and favorite quotes. Make a daily habit to write down all positive things that happened within the last 24 hours.

4. Brainstorm and make a list of the positive habits you are going to commit to over the next 30 to 90 days. Create a plan of action and get started immediately.

5. Take a daily walk to get some sunlight, decrease stress, and elevate your mood as you spend some time in nature. Take 10 deep breaths in your nose and out your mouth. Embrace the peaceful vibrations and reflect positive thoughts.

> "You are what you eat, physically and mentally. Make sure you pay close attention to what you consume."

Own Your Thoughts

I have learned over the years as a coach, mentor, and advisor that people are limited more by negative thoughts and attitudes than the opportunity itself. This is especially true when faced with adversity, stress, and anger.

Your negative thoughts are causing you to self-sabotage and derail your focus. It is imperative for your physical and mental well-being that you take control of your thoughts.

One little negative thought can grow and develop into something that spirals out of control. Some effects of negative thinking include lower self-esteem, anger, frustration, and depression. What you think becomes your reality. You own your thoughts.

The good news is: one small positive thought can grow into something great, far beyond the initial thought. Choose your thoughts wisely, and remember you can always create a new thought if one does not serve you.

Happiness is one of the greatest effects of positive thinking. To be happy, think happy, have positive thoughts, and watch your perception of life change right before your eyes. Your perception becomes your reality. Begin to create ways to think positively and watch how your life will change.

SOMETHING TO REMEMBER:

Stay focused and locked in on your goals. If you don't have a goal and a plan get one. Map it out. It is time to live on purpose.

NOW, GO BE THE GREATEST YOU.

CHAPTER 3

FIND YOUR WHY & SET A GOAL

My Connection.

I did a huge disservice to me for years. I undermined myself because I was not focused on my why or set setting goals. I lost countless hours because I was hoping and wishing and not planning to execute. I have cost myself thousands of dollars and hours due to my poor goal setting, undisciplined thinking, and lack of focus on my purpose.

I remember having a dream of being a millionaire, but I did not have a plan. I was truly dreaming. I was hustling without a real purpose or cause. I was looking for a way to get paid, but I didn't have a solid plan to help me reach my goals.

When I mapped out my goals and objectives, I could elevate and go to the next level. Without a goal, staying motivated was my biggest challenge.

When my first child was born, my why and purpose became illuminated. I had a new set of goals and a new sense of purpose. This new focus and purpose are still driving me to this day.

As I leveraged my newfound purpose in fatherhood, I still needed a plan. I started to map out the future for my kids, and we started to create plans for their future. I wanted my kids to be more successful than me. I was motivated because I had a clear goal.

Fast forward about 8 years after my firstborn, I was hit with a different motivation. I was not only the father of a daughter with 3 sons. Then I was hit with the unthinkable, that dreaded word… cancer. All my goals and plans shifted. I went from working to establish my family financially to fighting for my life. My motivation and purpose completely changed. I wanted to live and be around my kids more than I wanted to leave them a bunch of money. I knew time was more important than money, so my goals evolved.

As I started my journey to defeat cancer, I had to decide what I was working towards. I had to realign my goals and redefine my why. Keeping in proper perspective the reason I was fighting to beat cancer gave me the fuel I needed to push through the tough time. There have been days when I felt defeated by the treatment and the pain I was going through. When I thought about seeing my youngest son learn to walk and talk or seeing my daughter graduate high school, I locked my mind in on winning and beating cancer.

Without having a clear goal to be cancer free, I would not have come up with a definitive plan to defeat cancer. I would have just taken a defeated mindset which was a big threat to my life. By locking in on why I wanted to beat cancer, I could do things I never thought I would do. From vegan fast, no sugar diets, and fever baths to the hyperbaric chamber sessions, I was locked in because I had a goal and a purpose. I knew exactly why I was doing what I did.

If my case, cancer forced me to focus on why it was vital to live a certain way. I was forced to adjust my goals and lifestyle. Had I set the right goals and focused on my purpose to live a long healthy life before I for cancer, I could have possibly avoided a cancer diagnosis. I was forced to make a change. You don't have to be. You can set your goals and lock in on your purpose today.

What can we do? My Objective perspective.

Goal setting is part of our reality. We set objectives for our vacations, our well-being, and our lives as a rule. It appears that the present-day culture is continually pushing us to consider higher achievements.

A lot of people feel like they aren't getting anywhere in life. They put the work in but remain at a standstill.

It can be said that they feel this way because they haven't taken the time to think about what they want to do in life. They have not identified them, but why? It is harmful because everyone should think about that if they want to get somewhere in life and not waste their time. What is your why? What is your purpose?

It's anything but difficult to lounge around and figure out what we could do or what we'd prefer to do. It is a unique thing to acknowledge the compromises that accompany our objectives. Everyone wants a gold award. Not many individuals want to prepare like an Olympian.

Setting a goal is an incredible tool to bring your ideas to life so that they fit in your future the way you want them to.

If you set goals for yourself, then you have a clear-cut picture of your life in front of you. You will work towards it every day and willfully eliminate every interruption that can cause you to compromise on your goal or stray away from it.

When you are not purpose-focused, you can be easily distracted.

But to focus on your purpose, first, you need to know what you want to do. Once you have an idea of it and you know your goal for sure, then you should start to work towards it. Cross off every goal as you accomplish one.

All the people who are now successful in life set goals for themselves. If you want to be successful like them, you should start setting goals for yourself. Setting up goals gives you a lifetime supply of motivation and inspiration. It helps you to build your dream life.

When you set clear-cut goals for yourself, you will be able to see them through as well. You will accomplish them and feel a sense of achievement. You will know what you want and will flourish eventually. It will also help to boost your self-confidence and eradicate self-doubt.

You set your objectives in these ways:

First, you come up with a big picture in your head. You get an idea of how you want your life to look and what you want to accomplish in your life.

Then, you break down all your goals and carefully choose which goals you want to carry out. Select them and come up with an arrangement.

Finally, when you have your deliberately chosen goals and plans ready and by your side, start working towards them.

This is exactly why people always suggest looking at the broader view so that you can see which results will last for a long time and which will last for a short time. The things that you can see yourself doing even five or ten years later are the ones that you should pick now.

Coaching Support Questions:

These journal questions can help you clarify your goals, prepare for challenges, and stay accountable to your aspirations. Effective goal setting involves both thoughtful planning and ongoing assessment, and journaling can be a valuable tool to support this process.

Defining Your Goals:
- What are your top three short-term (1-3 months), medium-term (6-12 months), and long-term (1-5 years) goals?
- Why are these goals important to you? How do they align with your values and aspirations?
- What specific actions can you take in the next week to start working towards your short-term goals?

Progress Tracking and Adjustments:
- Regularly review your progress toward your goals. What milestones have you achieved, and what setbacks have you faced?
- Are there any adjustments or refinements you need to make to your goals or action plans based on your recent experiences and insights?
- Celebrate your successes, no matter how small, and use setbacks as opportunities to learn and grow.

Overcoming Challenges:
- Identify potential obstacles or challenges you may encounter while pursuing your goals.
- How can you proactively plan to overcome these challenges or mitigate their impact?
- Consider seeking advice or support from mentors, friends, or resources to help you navigate potential roadblocks.

Recommended Action Item.

Create a BE SMART Goal. This is slightly different from the standard or traditional SMART goals.

Brainstorm - Take time to brainstorm and think your way through each situation. Think of all the ideas, plans, and options and write them down. No idea is a bad idea. The more ideas you have, the better. You can refine your list later. Get all of the information and thoughts outside of your mind. Get them onto paper or some form of record keeping. Prioritize your goals based on what you want to accomplish first. Write it down.

Enthusiasm Energy - Look at your ideas. What makes you excited the most? What do you have the energy to do? Check your energy and see if you have the enthusiasm and mental stamina to go the distance. If not, go back and brainstorm ideas until you find the one that excites, inspires, and motivates you. If you choose something that you are not enthused about, you are more likely to quit. Find your passion and check your energy before you move on.

Specific - Be very specific about what you want to achieve. If you are not certain, go back to the brainstorming session until you are certain. What exactly do you want to accomplish?

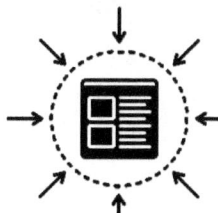
If you are writing a book, what are the name, type, and content? Starting a business? Name, type, location, services.

Are you going back to school? When, where, degree?

Be very specific about what you want. General is not good enough.

Measurable - Put in place a way to measure the effectiveness. Put in benchmarks as you go, so you track your progress. What can you measure to track your success?

How many pages did you write in that book this week? What is the schedule for completion? Are you on target or not? What adjustments need to be made?

Applicable Action - Take the appropriate time to map out your actions. If you are taking actions that don't serve your purpose, adjust your efforts to support your goal. Keep a mental and physical track of your efforts and time. What are the actions that you can take that will apply directly to your goals?

Are you taking those actions?

What else needs to be done to help advance your mission?

Avoid time and money wasters. Find the daily task and only do the things that advance your mission.

Represent - Make sure the goals represent your core values. If you are setting goals that are not ethical, moral, or in line with your purpose, rethink. What is the most respectable and honorable thing you can do to help power you towards your goal?

What are your core values? Write them down. Are your goals in line with your values?

Are you being represented the right way in pursuit of your goals? How do you know?

Timely - Set a specific deadline for each goal you set and break the big goals into smaller goals. Make sure you review deadlines and set timely checkpoints.

What is the deadline you have set for your goals and objectives?

How many checkpoints do you have?

30? 60? 90? Days?

What happens if you don't reach goal by the deadline?  your

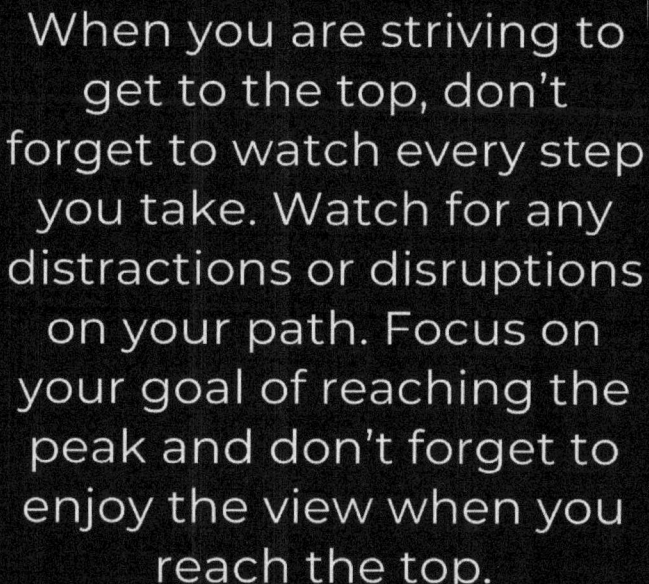

SOMETHING TO REMEMBER:

When you are striving to get to the top, don't forget to watch every step you take. Watch for any distractions or disruptions on your path. Focus on your goal of reaching the peak and don't forget to enjoy the view when you reach the top.

NOW, GO BE THE GREATEST YOU.

CHAPTER 4

MASTER FOCUS MANAGEMENT

My Connection.

I used to think that getting things done was about time management. I felt if I could master time, I could be at the top of my game. For some reason, it always seemed like there was not enough time in the day to get anything done. Man, if I could just have more time, I could do it all, I thought.

Then something happened. The world was hit by a pandemic. Our entire world came to a standstill. I was gifted with the one thing I had wanted for years, time. I was working from home, with no commute, and had more time than I knew what to do. At that moment, I had self-realization.

As I struggled to get things done, finish my website, and develop my business plan, I realized it was not a lack of time. It was a lack of focus. I had to admit, I am somewhat of a scatterbrain and can be all over the place. In those moments, my lack of focus has cost me thousands of dollars and hours. Even sitting down and writing this book took longer than it should have because of constant distractions and consistent focus.

I had to learn how to put aside the things that distracted me from focusing on the things that moved me closer to my goal. It's a never-ending process. I am still on my journey to master focus management and the need was highlighted again with my cancer diagnosis.

When I was diagnosed with cancer, I was greeted with a ton of medical information and sympathy from people who cared for me. I was overwhelmed with doctor visits and people offering their opinions. The more I listened to all the information and entertained certain conversations, the more distracted I became. Without finding what to lock in and focus on, I would have been stressed and distracted marching towards death.

After I took some time to study my cancer and what it was doing inside of my body, I charted my path and worked to find the right plan and lock in. I knew that if I allowed distractions to knock me off course, it could be a threat to my life. my goal was to focus on the controllable and do what I could do and not focus on what I could not. My first plan of action was to focus on exercise and diet. along with my cancer diagnosis, I was also prediabetic. The first target was to get my weight under control. I locked in and went into hyper-focus mode.

My first goal was to walk 10,000 steps per day. I figured if cancer was trying to break my body down, I needed to do what it takes to build it back up. Even though it was summer in Arizona and very hot, I found a way to push past all distractions and stay focused. I knew the weather would always provide the opportunity to make an excuse, but I was locked in and focused. If I could not go outside, I would create a walking path inside my house or take a trip to a local mall or big department store. I was so locked in on my goal to beat cancer, that I was not going to allow a heat wave or a dust storm to distract me.

To complement the walking and exercise, I also made extreme diet changes as part of my cancer battle. This was one of the hardest adjustments because I spent years programming bad habits, and it was not easy to make the adjustments even though my life was on the line. I had to make some hard choices and keep my mission to be cancer-free top of mind. My new diet required a ton of focus because I was used to eating recklessly and with a ton of undisciplined thought.

My first target in my diet change was sugar. I loved sugar and consumed it constantly until I heard it feeds cancer. I think cut it out completely for months. I locked in on cutting sugar and adjusting my diet and the temptations kept coming. My wife and kids did not join me in any sugar fast and they constantly consumed the foods of my past around me. I could not focus on what they were eating or doing. I had to lock in on my diet and do what it took for me to reach my goal of being cancer free. Anytime I got tempted, I would think about the cancer cells growing inside with each bite and my life being cut short because of a lack of discipline. It has not been an easy journey but my desire to beat cancer is stronger than my desire to satisfy a sweet tooth.

Cancer made me adjust and reinforce my focus. Find the catalyst you need to help keep you on track. Lock in and focus on your goal. Anything that doesn't support your goal is a distraction that needs to be eliminated.

What can we do? My Objective Perspective.

Going back to the previous chapter, you have set goals for yourself. Now, it's time to execute them with laser focus.

Carrying out a goal doesn't mean just carrying it out. To be able to do this, there is something that you need to do that will help carry it out the way that you planned.

And for that, you need to focus. All your attention should be on your goal and nowhere else. Your undivided attention will help you achieve all your goals and give you a sense of self-discipline as well, along with other positive attributes. You will work faster and harder if you focus on your goal and stop wandering.

Perhaps the quickest approach to gain ground on your objectives is to just press stop on less important things and spotlight each objective in turn. In some cases, you need to rearrange your needs slightly, and unexpectedly, progress comes considerably more rapidly because you are currently completely dedicated to an objective, just getting moderate consideration beforehand.

This is a powerful understanding. Commonly, when we neglect to arrive at our goals, we think something wasn't right with our objective or our methodology. The truth is, "You need to think greater! Pick a big goal that is so huge it will spur you consistently." Don't entertain thoughts like, "If only there were more than 24 hours in one day!" There is not. We can't increase the time but we can increase the focus.

a lack of focus clouds the objective and presents greater issues. What frequently resembles an issue of goal setting is an issue of goal choice. What we truly need isn't greater goals; however, we need a better core interest. You need to pick a certain something and mercilessly wipe out everything else and simply focus.

When the time comes when you have accomplished a goal, try to take a moment when you think about the hard work you did and marvel at your work to feel motivated to do even more tasks.

If the task that you did was a little bit harder, then reward yourself with something. This acknowledgment is important for your self-assurance and confidence.

After having accomplished the mentioned objective, now audit the remainder of your objective plans:

On the off chance that you accomplished the objective too effectively, make your next objective harder.

If a task was hard and required more effort, make sure that the next task you complete is easier in comparison.

On the off chance that you did something that would induce a change in your objectives, don't hesitate.

If you failed to reach your goal, rearrange your approach towards that task a little so that you can do it better next time.

Coaching Support Questions:

1. What do you do to help keep you focused? Write it down.

2. When you get distracted, how do you refocus yourself? Write it down.

3. What is going on in your life that requires the most focus? Write it down and keep it posted so you can read it.

Effective Time Management:
- Track how you allocate your time throughout a typical day or week. What activities or tasks consume the majority of your time?
- Assess whether your time allocation aligns with your priorities and long-term goals. Are there areas where you could better invest your time?
- Experiment with time management techniques, such as the Pomodoro Technique or time blocking, and journal about how these strategies impact your ability to stay focused.

Understanding Your Distractions:
- Reflect on your typical sources of distraction throughout the day. What are the common triggers that divert your attention?
- Are there specific times or environments where you find it particularly challenging to stay focused?
- Consider listing your top three distractions and brainstorming strategies to minimize or eliminate them.

Mindfulness and Focus Building:
- Explore mindfulness practices, such as meditation or deep breathing exercises. How do these practices affect your ability to concentrate and manage distractions?
- Reflect on moments when you were in a state of flow, completely absorbed in a task. What factors contributed to this state of heightened focus?
- Create a daily mindfulness or focus-building routine, and track your progress over time. How does consistent practice influence your ability to manage your attention effectively?

Recommended Action Item.

Development of Action Activities:

1. Track your life for a week. Each week has 168 hours. Keep a detailed account of every second if possible. Write down the time you go to sleep, wake up, and all things in between. Look at the amount of time that you spend on each task. Find the wasted time and reallocate it the following week to get more done.

2. Prep your lunch for the week on Sunday and lay out all of your outfits for the workweek. Find a shortcut that you can do today that will save you time the following day. Find one momentum-building activity you can do today that will benefit you tomorrow.

3. Gather the human capital needed to complete the task and work on delegation skills by assigning and trusting others who will get the job done. Focus strictly on your part of the team assignment.

4. Practice mindfulness. Find a quiet spot, set a timer for 30 seconds and to one minute. Just focus on your breathing and nothing else--in your nose and out of your mouth. Listen to the sound of the air and try to make each breath the same.

SOMETHING TO REMEMBER:

Don't worry about yesterday. Don't think about tomorrow. Focus on today because that's all you have. Don't overlook the joy of today in search of something and a day that may never come. Lock in on your Greatness and don't ever compromise your happiness.

NOW, GO BE THE GREATEST YOU.

CHAPTER 5

DO NOT COMPROMISE

My Connection.

Disclaimer: In any relationship or partnership, a certain amount of compromise must exist for progression. Healthy compromise is needed and deemed appropriate in most healthy relationships. When I speak of not compromising, it is strictly from a values system goal and aspiration perspective.

I am guilty of compromising more than I should have. I remember having personal goals, and I let people talk me out of my mission. People would question me, and I would begin to question myself. I would then reshape what I was thinking and the actions that followed.

Every time I look back on the times I have compromised, it puts in perspective why I haven't reached my biggest and wildest dream. I was afraid of failure and judgment, and as a result, I would compromise my goals and play it safe. If I had taken more risks and been more confident previously, I could have put myself in a better position.

As I have gotten older, I have learned not to compromise my happiness and positive mindset personally. I have been guilty of doing that in the past. I have compromised my happiness for other people and been in toxic environments longer than I should.

These days I have a goal never to compromise my happiness or my positive mindset. There have been times when I have been down and depressed mentally. In those moments, I set personal goals to build up my mind to have some emotional reserve when those dark moments hit. It's a daily journey.

I have been around certain co-workers and friend circles who loved to gossip about things around the office. I would refuse to listen or participate because, at this point, I set a personal goal for myself to keep me mentally focused. Before you know it, the gossipers would take their negativity and chatter elsewhere.

Even though I refused to join the gossip, I often became the focus of their gossip. That was and is perfectly fine with me as long as the gossip doesn't compromise my happiness, desire to stay positive, or ability to reach my goals.

There are some people I have known for years, and I had to sever my connection because certain aspects of our relationship compromised certain values I seek to maintain and the goals I set for myself. Once my focus was locked in, it became easier to recognize things that are considered distractions.

The more you compromise, the easier it is to continue and form the unhealthy habits of compromising yourself. Don't compromise your values, goals, or your desire to be great.

During my cancer battles, I was faced with many options and advice. After dealing with the negative side effects of chemotherapy treatment, I was in search of other treatment options. I quietly started my search for something to help build up my body and mind. I found a natural path that I wanted to take. After taking the time to research and put together my action plan, I shared my plans with my team including my doctors and my wife. They were convinced that chemo was the best for me. I could tell it was breaking me down and the side effects were worse than cancer.

I decided to go all in to build up my body. I committed to a program in Colorado that was very mentally and physically challenging. When I made my commitment, there was so much pushback from my team including my wife and doctors. While I respected their input, I knew it was my body and choice. I was going through the chemo and not them. I decided to lock all the way compromise on my goal and choose the path to defeat cancer. It created some tense moments, but I was locked in and not willing to compromise on what I felt was best for me and my future.

As a result of my focus and refusal to compromise, I was able to stop the cancer growth, strengthen my body, and jump-start a path to beating cancer. I fully understand the medical professionals and my loved ones didn't mean any harm with their suggestions and recommendations. They made the best recommendation based on what they knew. There were some difficult conversations and uncomfortable moments but at the end of the day, I stuck to what I felt was right. I didn't compromise with my decision. I truly believe if I would have compromised my goals, my ending would have been different, and I might not be here.

What can we do? My Objective perspective.

When it comes to choosing a goal for yourself, you should not hold back. You should paint a perfect picture in your head and don't shy away from it under any circumstances. Do not compromise on achieving it, and do not think that maybe I can't do this after all. Know exactly which ideal life you want and work towards it without ever doubting yourself. Compromise is not an option and not something that you can or should ever afford.

To do that, start with your profession and business. Think about both and then your ideal life. Then, answer these questions:

- What would it look like?
- What would you be doing?
- Where would you be doing it?

At the point when it's inside your capacity, work when you are in simply the most profitable form, regardless of whether that is promptly in the first part of the day, during the evening, or late around evening time.

Discover what your most profitable hours in the day are. On the off chance that you discover you are most engaged when you

work from 12 a.m. to 2 a.m. (also, you telecommute or can push off work to those occasions), at that point, everything implies doing as such!

If your work-life balance likes to work somewhat consistently, at that point, do as such.

It is critical to be a working citizen, so ensure you fit your different needs into your timetable. Be that as it may, don't modify your needs for another person who has no say in your life and lifestyle.

Now and again, you need to make quick amends on the off chance that you need to be experienced long-haul adjustments. Get up an hour sooner, work during lunch, and skip time viewing a film.

On the off chance that you have a fantasy you're seeking after external your Monday-Friday work, don't feel constrained to chip away at it during typical business hours.

Work to your cadence; however, make it certain that you work and keep doing it.

You must be the main individual to esteem and regard your time. Set limits so you can achieve important things. If you don't, at that point, nobody else will.

Your needs, objectives, and dreams should start things out in your timetable, sensibly speaking.

Everybody's circumstance is extraordinary. If you have a family, you need to impart your chance to those individuals who matter most. On the off chance that you work distantly, you can be more childish with your time. However, at some level, we need to get narrow-minded with our work opportunities.

On the off chance that you would prefer to peruse a book, study your opposition, or become familiar with your industry while your friends stare at the TV, at that point everything implies such. Pick exercises that will draw you one stage nearer to your dreams. Don't lose focus on that goal.

On the off chance that you plan on achieving your fantasies and accomplishing an enormous measure of achievement all the while, the key is to get extremely narrow-minded with your time. It is your time. It should be esteemed because it is one thing we can't accept a greater amount of one thing we can never get back.

Coaching Support Questions:

1. What are the values that you are not willing to compromise? Write them down.

2. What can you do to reset if your values are compromised? How do you start again? Create a list of

3. What can you cut out or back off on to make sure you don't compromise your dreams? Chart your reading material and time.

Identifying Potential Compromises:
- What are some situations or circumstances in which you have been tempted to compromise your goals in the past?
- Are there any recurring obstacles or challenges that have derailed your progress toward your goals?
- Consider your values and priorities. Are there any areas where you're willing to be flexible, and where do you firmly stand your ground?

Clarifying Your Goals:
- Are your current goals clear and well-defined, both short-term and long-term?
- Do you have a written plan or strategy for achieving your goals?
- How do your goals align with your values and long-term aspirations?

Maintaining Accountability and Resilience:
- How do you hold yourself accountable to your goals on a daily, weekly, or monthly basis?
- When faced with external pressures or distractions, how can you build resilience and stay committed to your goals?
- Reflect on past instances where you successfully resisted compromising your goals. What strategies or mindset shifts were instrumental in your success?

Recommended Action Item.

1. Make a list of your personal goals. List the people whom you can depend on or leverage to help guide you personally. Contact those people to build a personal mastermind of people who will build you up.

2. Make a list of your professional goals. List the people whom you could depend on to help guide you professionally. Contact those people who build a professional mastermind of people who will build you up.

3. Choose one main goal or objective and focus on doing something to advance that goal daily for 21 days. Make sure to set aside a specific time or amount of time to work on the project. Make sure you don't compromise or let anything interfere with your objective for three weeks.

"Don't get your dreams compromised by sharing them with people who are not qualified to help you accomplish them."

SOMETHING TO REMEMBER:

Today is a new day. New ideas, new opportunities and new levels to reach. No need to get caught up on the old when you have a new fresh start daily. Time to prepare for the new by releasing the old. New levels await. It's time.

NOW, GO BE THE GREATEST YOU.

CHAPTER 6

FIND YOUR MOTIVATED TRIBE

My Connection....

I am very particular about whom I invest my time these days. I can't always say that was the case. There were times when I allowed myself to be influenced and compromised by the thoughts and opinions of other people.

The phrase: you are what you eat not only refers to what you put in your mouth and what you put in your mind. A lot of that has to do with the people you choose to surround yourself with. Even though some people are good friends with relationships that go back years, they can still not be the best people for you to be around when it is time to make your power play.

I have some people who have been part of my life for decades. Our relationship goes back to childhood. I love them as people, but that can be pessimistic. For years I entertained them because they are good people, and our relationship has tenure. When it came down to it, I was not gaining value beyond a check to make sure people I cared about were ok. When it came to my business and personal goals, these people were not the go-to people I needed to elevate my business.

I decided to seek out my tribe. As a speaker and coach, I needed to be around people who were doing things beyond my current position. On an average day, I was not around enough people who were motivated and inspiring me to do be and be greater.

I invested in becoming a member of the Next Level Speaking Academy. I joined a team full of motivated speakers and aspiring coaches who were doing the things I dreamed of doing. I could not share my dreams and aspirations with groups of people because they have the same personal vision. As a part of this network, I could see the results, which motivated me to elevate my work ethic. Being around the right tribe empowered me to grow beyond my comfort zone. I had the permission to go all in and be the greatest version of myself.

I had a personal goal of making $50,000 per month. If I told someone who was only making $5,000, those individuals might perceive my desire to be far-fetched. They might even think I was a bit obsessive or materialistic. They might not understand my desire to create generational wealth for my kids.

When I speak to people who consistently make $100,000 per month, they would say-- absolutely, you can do that and much more. That gave me the confidence I needed to reach the next level.

I learned that you must find your audience and support system when you are on certain missions. Good people can give bad advice and have a negative perspective. Don't get caught up listening to the wrong people because they are friends or family. The people we love the most can still be negative and limited in their thinking and perspective.

Don't be afraid to do as I did. Find

your tribe, even if it means investing financially in yourself and your dreams. Don't settle for what you have. Get out there and find your tribe. You are not alone and others are ready to reciprocate your energy.

What can we do?

My Objective Perspective.

Have you ever met one of those individuals who consistently is by all accounts empowered and excited — as though they had a mystery supply of motivation?

The individuals we encircle ourselves with sway us significantly. Profoundly energetic individuals utilize this for their potential benefit. In little, regular associations, you most likely acknowledge how much effect others can have on your degrees of inspiration:

One positive cooperation with a strong and eager companion can supercharge your energy and inspiration in a flash. On the other hand, only one associated with a truly adverse, basic individual can deplete you of energy and sap your inspiration for the afternoon.

Be that as it may, there's a greater guideline here:

The individuals you constantly invest energy with influence how you routinely feel. On the off chance that you need to associate reliably with energy-depleting individuals, you can't anticipate feeling vigorous and energetic consistently. In any case, on the off chance that you constantly communicate with energy-giving individuals, you can't resist the urge to have a portion of their excitement and inspiration come off on you.

So be insightful about the

individuals you decide to invest your energy with:

If you're going after another position, take a glimpse at the energy levels of the individuals you'll be working with.

If you are beginning another venture or business with somebody, attempt to discover somebody who gives you energy.

Also, on the off chance that they don't, their different resources should be truly justified, despite all the trouble!

On the off chance that you need to feel more inspired and empowered in your life, encircle yourself with energy-giving individuals.

Coaching Support Questions:

1. Who is in your motivational circle? Make a list of all the people who keep you on track.

2. How often do you communicate with the people who motivate you? Create a schedule to communicate with your support team.

3. What value do you add to the people who motivate you to keep the relationship reciprocal? Map out the value you add to your support group to ensure they are refreshed throughout the process.

Exploring Potential Communities:
- What are some communities, groups, or organizations that align with your interests and aspirations?
- Have you already identified any potential tribe members within your existing network?
- Consider online platforms, local clubs, or events that could help you connect with like-minded individuals. How can you actively engage with these opportunities to build your tribe?

Defining Your Ideal Tribe:
- What specific qualities, values, or interests do you believe are essential for your ideal tribe members to share?
- Reflect on your personal and professional goals. How can your tribe members contribute to your growth and elevation?
- List three characteristics or attributes you would like to see in your tribe members, and explain why each is important to you.

Nurturing Relationships and Mutual Growth:
- Once you start building your tribe, how do you plan to nurture these relationships for mutual growth and support?
- What can you offer to your tribe members in return for their support and encouragement?
- Reflect on past experiences where you've been part of a supportive community. What lessons can you apply to foster a positive and elevating tribe environment?

Recommended Action Item

1. ***Get a support partner-*** Many of us get down on ourselves because of the little negative person who lives in our heads. The person can be very negative and discouraging, which has a tremendous effect on our self-confidence. To combat the negativity, sometimes we have to rely on other people's beliefs until our faith in ourselves is restored. Find a positive support partner or group and build your little motivation accountability circle. Supporting each other is the bridge we need to help us cross the valley of self-doubt.

2. ***Take inventory of your circle-*** look at all of the people in your immediate circle. Analyze how you interact with each person. Whom do you visit to vent? Whom do you motivate? Who motivates you? Who is adding value, and who is not? Contact the people who motivate and inspire you and thank them.

3. ***Motivate somebody else-*** Find someone in your circle who is not the most positive and offer them some positive words and affirmations. Send them a weekly text with positive words. Help cultivate your positive circle.

4. ***BONUS TIP-*** Invest in a group or become part of a

network that is doing what you want to do already. Become part of a tribe designed to do what you are speaking to do. Don't be afraid to INVEST financially if you need to. Your dreams and goals are worth it.

"The Value of connecting and working with a tribe of motivated, like-minded individuals working towards a common goal is so underrated."

Quentin O. Henry.

SOMETHING TO REMEMBER:

What's for YOU is for YOU and nothing can stop that. Replace concern and worrying with rejoicing and celebrating. Your next level awaits. Sending my Congrats in Advance. You got this.

NOW, GO BE THE GREATEST YOU.

CHAPTER 7

TAKE BREAKS WHEN NECESSARY

My Connection.

My go-to move was always to grind all day and all night. I felt that hard work and the grind was the way. My mindset became I don't sleep, I grind. I would spend all my time locked in. I even felt guilty for not working and taking too many breaks. I learned the hard way; I was wrong.

I got burned out from going all-in for years, and I still didn't have the results I was seeking. At first, I thought I just needed to work even harder to get to my goals, and I went back to working even harder. I found that I was still not making progress. Truthfully, I was too tired to have optimal focus.

One day, I had a realization. I was working on a book and program. I sat at my desk for hours, grinding away until I ran into a roadblock. I was having a hard time organizing my thoughts and articulating my vision. I went to bed tired and frustrated. The next day when I woke up, my mind and body were both refreshed. I was able to do more in 30 minutes than I could do in hours the day before. At that moment, I realized that for years I was doing it wrong.

Certainly, there are times when grinding and pushing through are needed to get your dreams and goals moving; but rest and breaks are just as important. Many people felt like me and felt that guilt for resting and taking time off. The truth is our minds and bodies need a certain amount of rest to perform at their best.

To increase my productivity, I had to learn how to take healthy breaks to keep me performing at an optimal level. I could not give all my time and energy to my plans and goals and not appreciate what was already in front of me.

As I was working on this chapter, my one-year-old son came over and stood next to me. At that moment, I felt it was important to take a break. There have been many times I would have sent my kids away or given them a virtual babysitter. Now I realize that in many cases when they show up, I need to take a break.

Overworking until exhaustion used to be a badge of honor. Today, I take the time to rest up so I can show up to BE THE GREATEST.

What can we do?

My Objective Perspective.

Regardless of the amount you have on your plate, you must remember that you are not doing anybody in your life — including yourself — anything great by workaholic behavior.

Students look at how long they work in the present exhaust culture and the time put into restless evenings. Collaborators gloat about extra time. Companions gripe that they're busier than each other. You may even notice your family attempting to one-up one another with insane outstanding burdens over the supper table.

For many of us, workaholic behavior is viewed as excellent. Some trust it shows commitment or energy when all it truly does is make it harder for you to buckle down later.

Certain goals influence the nature of rest you get every night. Studying late at night has demonstrated the connection between long work hours and rest quality. Regardless of whether that is from high pressure, gazing at screens, or continually working psyche, your outstanding task at hand can contrarily influence your rest plan. We normalize trading in rest for higher achievement not realizing we could be doing the exact opposite.

However, a sound rest plan isn't the main thing exhausting impedes. When you grow negative behavior patterns like working until you nod off or pull dusk 'til dawn affair to complete things, it makes it harder for you to create more advantageous work propensities later. Also, this doesn't effectively assist your relationship with your work when all things considered.

Working in excess lifts your feelings of anxiety. In any case, it also solid restricts the measure of time you need to get exercise into your daily schedule or maybe an opportunity to prepare together a plate of mixed greens instead of choosing uptake.

The pressure brought about by workaholic behavior can likewise prompt negative adapting propensities from smoking, drinking liquor, or depending on medications to assist you with escaping work mode and into a condition of unwinding.

Stress and terrible methods for dealing with stress like these go inseparable. What's more, both of these can add to sorrow, tension, and other psychological sicknesses.

Notwithstanding long-haul harm to your psychological well-being, the remainder of your body won't thank you for those additional two hours at Moody. Individuals who work longer hours -are bound to experience the ill effects of various ailments and can create them before on throughout everyday life.

A recent report in the *Lancet Journal* presumed that the more drawn out the hours a representative worked, the higher the danger of experiencing a stroke or different types of cardiovascular illness. In a few different investigations from that point forward, exhaustion has been connected to a greater danger of creating diabetes and hypertension.

On the off chance that your well-being doesn't propel you to get some distance from your obsessive worker ways, the impact it has on your future work may persuade you. You are placing more work into something that doesn't improve the result.

Scientists have discovered that workaholic behavior can prompt more errors. The pressure and depletion of a stuffed timetable can make it significantly harder for somebody to do their everyday work. Indeed, an exhausting timetable significantly brings down the nature of work that can be created.

You can't transform anything, and it sincerely appears as though everybody is exhausting themselves now in their life. Even though no one is awesome, a portion of your friends may have a superior handle on adjusting their work-life and individual life than you.

There are numerous approaches to forestall wearing out what

might be more customized to you. Yet, some more broad ways to deal with forestalling burnout incorporate taking a break to accomplish something for yourself, defining limits between various pieces of your day, and denying added assignments when important.

Focus on the work you're doing well as opposed to distressing over future activities or past mix-ups. Zero in on one task right now without attempting to finish an excessive number of activities on the double. It is workable for the objective setting to hurt us if we set unreasonable goals that require a lot of us.

Sort out what's a solid work-daily routine equilibrium for you actually and experience that. Be sympathetic about what you're ready to manage without deciding about yourself. Be compassionate and cherishing toward yourself.

Ensure you have a lot of time to zero in on your physical and emotional well-being through exercise, treatment, and nurturing exercises. Set aside a few minutes for leisure activities and arrangements. Make time to have significant quality time with individuals you care about and who care about you. Give these exercises and individuals your full, full focus, and care.

It's essential to note that the busiest individuals aren't the most expertly or even scholastically effective. There's where working can begin to accomplish more mischief than anything.

You don't need to work 90 hours per week to propel yourself excessively hard. In a reasonable period, we should all be able to deal with various measures of work given the kind of work, our psychological well-being, our circumstance, and numerous different elements.

Coaching Support Questions:

1. What is your self-care plan? Write your plan down.
2. How often do you take to focus on your mental health?
3. What do you do to reset when you get burned out?

Understanding Your Energy Levels:
- How do you typically feel when you're low on energy or burned out? What are the physical, emotional, and mental signs?
- Reflect on your major goals. How has your energy level impacted your progress toward these goals in the past?
- Consider a recent day when you felt energized and productive. What activities or practices contributed to your high energy levels?

Balancing Work and Rest:
- Reflect on your current work habits. Are you prone to overworking or neglecting breaks in pursuit of your goals?
- How can you strike a balance between focused work and deliberate breaks to maintain consistent energy levels?
- Consider setting specific boundaries for work hours and break times. What changes can you make to ensure you prioritize your well-being and energy management?

Designing Effective Breaks:
- What are some strategies or activities that help you recharge and regain energy during breaks?
- How often do you currently take breaks throughout the day, and are they effective in rejuvenating you?
- Experiment with different break schedules (e.g., short breaks every hour, longer breaks every few hours) and journal about how each schedule affects your energy and productivity.

Recommended Action Item.

1. Set a reminder on your phone to remind you to take a break and go for a short walk. Even if you can't go outside, walk around the office or your home to get your blood pumping and clear your head.

2. Try meditation and mind relaxation activities. When we learn to control our minds, actions become more predictable, and we are in more control of our actions and results. Download an app or go to YouTube and look up videos.

3. Set a consistent time to go to bed and wake up. When you have steadiness, your body can become programmed to help you maximize your personal and professional performance. Don't push too many days without sticking to your schedule because you will

4. reprogram your body and mind with unhealthy habits.

"You are what you eat, physically and mentally. Make sure you pay close attention to what you consume."

SOMETHING TO REMEMBER:

It is time to step outside of that comfort zone. There is a lot that we have to accomplish in front of us and we can't do it by worrying about the things behind us. The time is now for us to elevate and celebrate. Get started. No one is going to do the work for you.

NOW, GO BE THE GREATEST YOU.

CHAPTER 8

KEEP TRYING. DON'T GIVE UP

My Connection.

Life will give us many reasons to give up, and I have personally taken advantage of those excuses. One of the main reasons I have stayed behind on certain goals is because I quit when I should have kept pushing—shame on me.

Now I realize that I can never give up; my mission and purpose become greater. When I was 17 years old, my aunt got me a job at her company the summer before my senior year in high school. This was one of my first jobs, and I was making "good money" for a high school kid at the time. I think it was about $6 an hour.

Each day, I had my pre-work routine. Since we lived next door to my grandparents, my Grandmother would always cook, so I would go to their house and get myself a plate before work. My Grandmother was not just a cook; she was a culinary master. She was the cook that other Grandmothers admired.

This one particular day, I was at my Grandmother's for my daily plate. As I lounged around the house, the time came for me to leave for work.

I had already made the decision that I was not going to work. On this day, we had an off-season football scrimmage against another team. Because this was my senior year, there was no way I was going to miss out on a team activity. As a leader, it was my duty to be there for my team during our senior year, even if it meant missing work and losing money.

Thinking back, my Grandmother said to me, "Ydrate, you better leave from here before you are late to work." I said, "Big Ma, I'm not going to work today; I'm going to football practice." At first, she didn't believe me. She repeated, "Boy get yo butt out here before you late." I confirmed that I was not going, she saw I was serious, and her tone changed.

Her face turned very serious, and she said, "Football practice. You are going to miss work for football practice?" I confirmed and explained that it was my senior year, and I was a leader, and I had to be there.

My Grandmother looked at me and said,

"Now Ydrate, those people gave you a job, and you took it. They gave you a chance and responsibility, and you are going to football practice. Look here, son; this is bigger than you. Somebody else believed in you and put their name on the line for you. They trusted you. And you are going to football practice. That is not what we do in this family. You go to work; you be responsible and work hard. Finish what you started. You can do football later when you are done."

Not the one to argue with Big Ma, I left her house, and I went straight to my friend Ike's house and hung out until football practice. After practice, I came home and was very quiet. My Grandmother could see our house out of her window, and if she saw my car home early, I would have some explaining to do.

About two hours later, there was a furious knock at the door. My mother and I both met at the door, and it was my Grandfather. His words were, "it's your Ma, I don't know if she is dead or what. At that point, my Mother and I just ran as fast as we could next door. She went in to try and revive my Grandmother as I called for help.

Ultimately, it was too late. My Grandmother passed away, and I was devasted. The one thing I will never forget from that was she told me to:

"Finish what you started."

I took that message, and I strive to live up to that standard each day. I want to encourage you to do the same thing. Finish what you start and never give up.

When cancer showed up in my life, the "never give up" theme became my mantra. I knew I was faced with mental and physical challenges. I realized that if my mindset was positioned on the negative, I would be more likely to be taken out by cancer growing in my body. There were days when my situation was getting the best of me, and I questioned my ability to beat cancer. In those days I had to dig deep inside of myself and encourage myself to never give up.

Some people had access to me who didn't have the same level of faith as me. They didn't believe and it felt as if they were giving up on me. Even when some of the people who should have been cheering me on gave up on me, I never gave up on myself. I embraced adversity and kept my faith. I am hopeful that my resilience and perseverance will inspire others to keep pushing.

What can we do?

My Objective Perspective.

As individuals, we all strive to BE THE GREATEST version of ourselves, making new companions, evolving ourselves, and so on. Despite the energy that an individual had when he or she chose to do something new, frustrations can restrain the expectation. In a circumstance like this, demoralization can happen. Sometimes, when we notice that something turns out badly and we falter to continue attempting.

In any case, what causes this demoralization?

Unquestionably, as of now, you are attempting to locate the correct answer, doing mental exploration, and considering the potential causes.

Regardless of this exertion, I ensure that you won't locate a definite answer since demoralization doesn't have an exact reason.

Be that as it may, attempt not to surrender. Keep on battling in any event, when all that is by all accounts against you. Activity implies change; change implies success! Achievement implies value; worth implies happiness! Disappointments make us more grounded and feature our solidarity and want to win.

Pursuing something is far superior to sitting ideal and contemplating failure. Life won't be in the way of joy; at times, you should feel distressed, then it makes you know the estimation of happiness. You ought not to get discouraged and continue going after your objectives. Disappointments are only one stage during accomplishing objectives.

Nobody can accomplish something without falling flat. A few people may have a couple of falls; however, others have more than that. So, don't burn through your important time by speculation about disappointments and attempt to take in something from that. Your prosperity would be at the highest point if you had more disappointments.

All the well-known innovators flopped repeatedly, yet never surrendered to it and proceeded with attempts with various techniques and gaining from others or various assets.

Any individual will confront disappointment at a specific time. However, this ought not to keep us from attempting once more. We should consistently step forward, paying little mind to the outcome. On the off chance that we don't win, in any event, we'll master something. Continue attempting in any event. What's more, when the issues come, how about we recall that any endeavor merits doing?

Attempt and attempt. One day you will get the achievement. This achievement and disappointment rely on your recognition, and on how you see things. It would help if you conceded these disappointments are venturing stones for your prosperity, and each time your disappointment gives you the occasion to gain from your errors. Trust so this time you get the achievement. Try to avoid panicking, don't get pushed, and make the most of your life.

Furthermore, what is the point in accepting that faltering isn't the point?

By trying and succeeding, you discover that you can do what you realized you could do.

By trying and coming up short, you realize what more you can do.

Succeeding and coming up short are not the point. Attempting is the point.

You shouldn't surrender since you have seen such a large number of disappointments or have seen others bomb too often in a similar industry or specialty you mean to seek after. Disappointment can also be a blessing in disguise. Every time you fall, it gives you a sense of maturity, and you rise even better than you ever did before.

Disappointment doesn't mean that you have failed badly. It just means your intended approach was not suitable.

Disappointment is the last objective of the plan you want to follow.

We, as a whole, have expectations and dreams. We think of the long haul and intend to accomplish the objectives — and begin pounding. We begin working crazy hours, have innumerable restless evenings, and push aside less important things. The gleaming light before us speaks to the objectives and persuades us to continue onward. In any case, now and then, we don't arrive given all the exertion. It can be a lot to deal with, disturbing, and agonizing.

The unendurable sensation of disappointment eats us from the inside and devours a few of us. We discard all that we've worked for and return to our regular daily existence, promising never to do it again. Regardless of whether we do, it will be something new and inconsequential to the bombed adventure.

However, it doesn't need to be like this. Disappointment doesn't speak to an absence of information, experience, or skill. It likewise doesn't mean we were insufficient or that we are not removed to be effective. All it is an impermanent mishap that shows us important things. Regularly, disappointment can be more gainful than progress on the main attempt.

Even though it could be hard to recuperate from disappointments, truth be told is a basic instrument to your prosperity. You gain a ton of proficiency when you lose; it is about the action, the cycle, and yourself. It assists with calling attention to the undeniable missteps, gaining from them, fixing them, and entering another endeavor with a new point of view. Accordingly, you have to dodge those mix-ups later on.

Another advantage you are getting is outrage and inspiration to vindicate yourself. The second most ideal approach to using the information you've gotten from misfortune is to lose control. Outrage gives you perseverance, inspiration, energy, and motivation. Also, since huge numbers of us feel that way, it's acceptable to transform a negative feeling into a good result.

On the off chance that you fizzled, gained from it, took a subsequent attempt, and lost again — it is anything but the motivation to self-destruct and surrender by the same token. Nobody guaranteed you would accomplish what you wish on the subsequent attempt. There is no guide to the number of shots you may need to get to your objective. It's diverse for everybody, and it relies upon numerous elements. Try not to search for somebody to reveal to you the number of endeavors you need to succeed — just shut up and continue crushing, regardless of whether it takes twelve attempts.

There is an almost negligible difference between requiring various endeavors and being a terrible fit. Perceive your shortcomings and break down how great you are in your endeavor. Some of the time, it very well may be a keen choice to change your objectives and change to an alternate way. Be that as it may, more often than not — continue hustling.

It's easy to feel discouraged and want to give up. But remember that you are still better than everyone else who hasn't even tried yet to achieve goals. Your failure doesn't define you. You are still very much capable of doing things. It was just a slip-up, nothing else. It is not a failure.

So, what's the mystery? Indeed, there isn't any. You simply need to continue attempting. Continue attempting.

Consequently, don't give up or feel down, regardless of how hard it will be. Continue attempting in any event, when you come up short, and the outcomes will amaze you.

Coaching Support Questions:

1. What is your biggest challenge right now? Write it down.

2. What are you doing to overcome your biggest challenge? Write out a detailed plan.

3. What do you do when you don't reach your goal and want to give up? Create a mental and put together your strategy beforehand.

Revisiting Your Dreams:
- What are the dreams or aspirations that have been the most important to you throughout your life?
- Reflect on the reasons why these dreams matter to you. How do they align with your values and long-term vision for yourself?
- Have your dreams evolved or changed over time? If so, how have they transformed, and why?

Creating a Resilient Mindset:
- Describe the mindset or attitude that you believe is essential for never giving up on your dreams.
- How do you handle self-doubt, criticism, or moments of discouragement? What strategies or self-talk help you stay motivated and resilient?
- Consider setting small, achievable milestones that lead toward your larger dreams. How can these milestones provide a sense of progress and encouragement along the way?

Overcoming Obstacles and Challenges:
- Think about the obstacles or setbacks you've encountered while pursuing your dreams. What were some of the most significant challenges you've faced?
- How did you react to these challenges? Did you persevere, adapt, or temporarily set your dreams aside?
- Reflect on past instances when you found the strength to keep going despite difficulties. What lessons can you draw from those experiences to apply to your current journey?

Remember that the pursuit of dreams often involves challenges and setbacks, but maintaining your focus and determination can lead to meaningful achievements. These journal questions can help you stay connected to your dreams, build resilience, and develop a mindset that supports your unwavering commitment to your aspirations.

Recommended Action Item.

1. **Post your goals** where you can see them each day. Read your short-term and long-term goals at least three times daily. Once in the morning when you get up. At least once during the day and another time before you go to bed. Set timers on your phone to remind you to review. Make sure you write down your goals. Look at them and read them out loud.

2. **Write a speech to yourself** that you would write to a friend if they came to you for inspiration during a downtime. What would you personally want to hear? Write it down in a speech format. What would you say to a friend? What would you want a friend to say to you?

3. **Surround yourself with tenacious people**. In your circle, you have some people who have mastered the art of never giving up. Leverage those relationships. These relationships might not be the same group of motivated friends. Having people close who are tenacious will give you an outlet and a source of inspiration to keep you moving forward.

10 Motivated Mindset Shifting Thoughts

1. All problems have solutions; all resources are delivered in divine timing.

2. Everything will work out for good.

3. There is a reason for everything under the sun.

4. Old situations with fresh perspectives lead to new solutions.

5. In every flaw, there is perfection.

6. Self-approval is a prerequisite for Greatness.

7. Giving up is the best way to waste ambition and a perfect transition to mediocre.

8. Coal without pressure means no diamonds.

9. The past has no power over the present and no influence on the future.

10. The rhythm and flow of the heart create the soundtrack for the journey to your destiny.

"You were created to be victorious. Don't undermine your Greatness by giving up on yourself. You can and will do it. Stay focused. "

SOMETHING TO REMEMBER:

Celebrate every single day or second for that matter. Life is short no matter how long we live. We have to embrace every moment and appreciate the good and the bad. They both work together. Plants need sun and rain in order to grow.

NOW, GO BE THE GREATEST YOU.

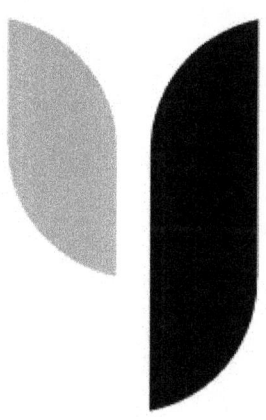

YDRATE NELSON

YDRATENELSON.COM

www.ingramcontent.com/pod-product-compliance
Lightning Source LLC
Chambersburg PA
CBHW071008160426
43193CB00012B/1966